Unlock the True Value of Your Own Business

Leveraging Time and Money to Have More of Both

Daniel T. Gardner

This book is not intended to be considered as financial, medical, legal or any other professional advice or service. The information provided is not a substitute for professional advice or care. If you desire or require financial, medical, legal or any other expert assistance, you should seek the services of a competent licensed and registered professional. The author, the publisher and their employees and agents are not liable for any damages arising from, or in connection with, the use of or reliance on any information in this book.

The material in this book may not be reproduced or transmitted in whole or in part in any medium (whether electronic, mechanical or otherwise) without the express written authorization of the author. To request authorization, please contact dan@dantgardner.com, outlining the specific material involved, the proposed medium, and, if applicable, the number of copies as well as the purpose of its use.

Dedication

To my wonderfully supportive wife, Susannah, I could not have done this without you in my corner. No matter how crazy I get, your unconditional love is my foundation. It gives me the confidence to just go for it.

To my son, Taylor, and daughter, Kelly, thank you for inspiring me to become the person I was always meant to be.

To my parents, thanks for making this possible in more ways than one.

To my coaches who are helping me through this transformation, Steve D'Annunzio, Conde Bartlett, Patti Keating and Veronika Noize, you will likely hear yourself in this book.

To Larry Plumb, Matt Mansfield and Roy Rasera, thanks for teaching me about world of personal finance.

To Becky Tengwall and all the "I Take the Lead" folks, thanks for helping me find my voice.

To Susan Rich, thanks for helping me start blogging and find the words to write this book.

To all the rest of my family and friends, thanks for your support, book suggestions, life lessons and all the other numerous ways you have contributed to my life.

I love you all.

Table of Contents

Foreword

Why write another book about success in business? I could not find the exact right blend of concepts and practical tips to fit my situation. I am a solopreneur striving to build a business in the conscious capitalist model. I currently have four coaches and have been on a reading frenzy, plus I love listening to entrepreneur's podcasts as they share their ideas.

Having spent more than 15 years in corporate America before taking the leap of faith into building my own business in 2011, I had witnessed the evolution of thought around how to get the most out of a corporate organization. Daniel Pink in **Drive** and Simon Sinek in **Start with Why** showed that people wanted to be inspired and fulfilled by becoming experts in their work and understanding why they were doing it. The problem is the dichotomy between the corporate quarterly profit reports and people working for said company wanting to be fulfilled. Even with the best intentions, boards of directors and CEOs have to respond to Wall Street. You hear the horribly inhumane words as your job is shipped off to somewhere else in the globe or even just to another division, "It is not personal, just business". These kinds of rationalizations have led to the destruction of the environment, putting workers in harmful situations and overall job dissatisfaction.

The corporate answer was to bring in the human resources professionals to talk about finding work/life balance. Of course, the CEO still wants you to spend all your time and effort on the company goals. I even had one CEO say that you could learn to play the violin or you could focus on your career. I strove to move upward. I sacrificed for my career while trying to be the father and husband I wanted to be. I worked hard and travelled the globe as an electrical engineer working in technical marketing and management roles. I enjoyed the customer and field engagements, but I felt unappreciated. While in college, I had worked commission sales for a big box retailer selling everything from electronics to appliances. As a part timer, I could make as much as the experienced full-time people. It was not about how hard you worked but how efficient you were and what relationships you built. Of course, the rules kept changing even then in order to motivate the sales force to accomplish the current corporate goals.

I must be a slow learner because it took me about 20 years of working to realize that I was an entrepreneur. I kept hoping someone would notice me and mentor me on how the world really worked. Lift me up and take me under their wing. I kept looking outside myself for the answers. Even worse, I needed the external acknowledgement of my value. I keep pushing myself and others to achieve more so that I'd be noticed for the next big promotion. It wasn't until I just couldn't take it anymore that I started to realize that I was my own biggest problem. It was not about someone else noticing me. It was about me BEING me. It was not about doing more. It was about doing the right things. It was not about blaming anyone else. It was taking 100% responsibility. It was not about beating myself up. It was about forgiveness and compassion, for others, and especially for myself.

I found most business success books were about process or systems to make more efficient use of time, energy and money. I found most self-help books were about finding the right relationships or losing weight or just being happy with a vision board and a couch. All these ideas have good nuggets in them. There are many good practical systems. Eventually you find some that work for a while, but then you out grow them. Why keep looking outside yourself for the answers? It is not about finding the right "how to" guide but a "why to" guide for yourself.

I've met a lot of really smart, caring and nice people. Most of them just accepted that life was just not fair. A few have decided they are going to change the world for the better and are seeking a way to do just that through unlocking their true value. This book is for you.

As my coach and friend Steve D'Annunzio likes to say before we embark on a multi-day symposium. I'm not going to say that any of this is true, but you might find parts of it useful. We are all in this life together and are all equals. Take the best and leave the rest. My own addition is that if you find something truly inspirational, share it with others. A great motto is to remember to "pay it forward".

Dan Gardner
West Linn, OR
Saturday, June 21, 2014

Chapter 1: Setting the Context

It is human nature to want to love and be loved. Most of us have been guilty of desperately seeking acceptance in our family and group of friends at one point in our lives. Part of trying to make our parents proud includes going to college and then finding a prestigious career. At some point, we realize that we are living out some societal ideal of success more so than our own. For me, it was finding a woman whom I truly love and who truly loves me. Actually, we were both busting our butts in pursuit of the American dream when children came along. That was the real turning point that led to me asking myself "why am I doing this?" Most parents strive to make their children's lives better than their own, usually trying to compensate for what they felt their parents could have done better.

My parents are abnormally normal. They've been married only once and are still happily married. They live in the same house that we moved into when moving to Oregon in 1973. My dad had a successful career as a physics professor and my mom as a teacher at the local community college. They retired into an entrepreneurial business, which does make them a bit strange. Growing up, we were never rich and money was often too precious to spend on fancy clothes, bikes or cars. We did have a vacation house at the beach and traveled, so there was some discretionary income. I have tons of fond memories of road trips to visit friends and family, trips to Europe and Hawaii, camping and of course the beach. Around town, my mom made sure we were involved in sports, music and other activities. We lived in a quiet college town, so we rode our bikes around everywhere. It was as close to perfect an upbringing as I could imagine for anyone.

My brother and I were taught that it is important to work hard. It was better to sacrifice a bit now for a better future. I felt I was in complete control of my future from an early age. I was going to work hard in school to get good grades, in order to get into a good college, in order to get a good job. With a good job, I'd have money to buy a nice house and car. I'd find a nice woman to marry and we'd have two kids and a wonderful life.

It worked, too, up to the point that I was at risk of missing once in a lifetime things in my own kids' lives. There is no value you can put on seeing the first babble from your son, or seeing your daughter take her first steps. As a parent, no one has to tell you that the world is bigger than you. You feel it in your gut and your soul. As these helpless creatures grow into walking, talking, smaller versions of you and your spouse, you don't want to miss a thing. You also don't want them to be without anything. Of course, you don't want to spoil them either. All the sudden, all I wanted from work was the pay check and spending as little time there as possible. I would sneak into the elementary school classroom before work to volunteer in the classroom. I would take a late lunch break to coach their sports teams or LEGO robotics. I began to really resent business travel that seemed more about activity than productivity. I wanted to be home unless it was for a damn good reason. I started asking more questions at work and expecting more of those around me. I didn't want to waste any time. I still wanted the business to be successful but I wanted to get my work done and get out of there.

There never seemed to be enough time. No one else seemed to care as much as I did or work as hard as I did. Any promotions or raises were too little, too late. I was stressed out, overweight and unhappy. I blamed those at work and my wife at home. The first time I was laid off, it was a crushing experience. After all I had done to try and save a failing product line over the past six years, I'm the one that is cut. How could they do that to me? My kids' were in onsite preschool so it was going to dramatically change our lives unless I found some other group to land in quickly. Luckily, I did. It was a bit of a demotion and that even seemed like a relief to not have the responsibility of management. I did make a decision to work on more projects that were directly tied to revenue and do things that I found fun. I worked on many cross-functional and cross-divisional projects. The frustrating thing was the silos between the business objectives of the overall global corporation and the product group. I really wanted to see the big picture and couldn't find anyone who seemed to have it. After accomplishing success in some big projects, it was almost a relief to get laid off again after four years.

I had the same three month severance package as four years earlier, except back then I never had to take it because I had landed the transfer in the less than two weeks thanks to the help of a good friend who made sure I talked to the right people in the new group. This time, I really couldn't muster the energy to try the internal transfer route again. I felt entitled after my accomplishments that someone would offer me a position in line with my status. I knew how the whole interview process worked in high tech and the last thing I wanted was to load up a resume full of the hot key words to the job website so some HR recruiter would find it in a search. I'd get the calls and try to sound excited as they wanted me to do some boring thing inside another giant corporation. I was either overly qualified or not exactly the right technical fit. **Office Space** was the perfect movie to explain how I felt. I felt like doing nothing would be the perfect job for me.

I didn't want to work for anyone. I wanted to have my own business. I also wanted to be part of something. While I wanted to have the flexibility to be there for my family, I wanted to get out of the house to work. I prided myself on my work ethic and sheer will to get things done. I didn't have capital to not make money for long or to buy a business. No one was looking for a CEO with no experience running a business. I needed to build something, AND quickly. I was frustrated with how much health insurance cost with COBRA from my recent employer so I started looking at that industry. I went to cattle call interviews at several firms. As I introduced myself and my varied background of technical, marketing and sales experience, a leader would usually pull me aside and tell me how much money we would make together. It seemed pretty slimy. I picked the one that seemed to fit me the best and started on my licensing. At that point, I thought about the financial services firm where I was a client.

My financial advisor was a longtime family friend and had introduced me to the president of his firm. I had been a client for seven years and had really loved the initial educational portion of the work we had done together. At one point, I remember the president telling me that if I ever wanted to work there, I'd be great at it. My friend and I had been working on a plan to give me the freedom to exit the corporate American rat race and to start my own business at some point. We were about three and half years into a five year plan. He wasn't too keen on me joining the business because of what he knew of my financial situation and what he knew about starting a financial services practice. Despite his objections, I did it anyway.

I had no choice but to succeed. My engineering salary was 2-3 times the average first year starting income in financial services. The income was performance based so it was up to me to sell enough to make what I needed for my family to maintain the current lifestyle. The first six months were tough with trying to launch a business as I completed getting all my licenses for the business lines I was told were important. I had the distinct advantage of being a client and had witnessed how the planning process worked, firsthand. In my first full calendar year, I did well. I ended up eighth in the nation for new representatives. At the end of the year, I realized that I was working even harder than I had before and I needed to find a better way.

I enjoyed having intimate conversations with people about their hopes and dreams for their family finances. I learned a lot about people and realized that I needed to learn more. The technical part of the job was interesting but it didn't matter how much I knew unless I could show potential clients how much I cared. I was talking to everyone I knew and hoping they'd introduce me to more people. I started going to networking events and joining networking groups. An acquaintance experienced in the financial services industry met me and recommended two books, **The Go-Giver** by Bob Burg and John David Mann and **Networking with the Affluent** by Thomas J. Stanley. Those two books really changed my life and ignited a thirst for self-discovery. Asking others what to read next, led me to **The Prosperity Paradigm** by Steve D'Annunzio and my first business coach.

This rambling introduction was hopefully helpful in setting the context in how I found myself here where I am today. For many of you may identify with my path. You probably recognize that my limiting beliefs are holding me back. As I became aware of them, I began searching for how to overcome them. In the following chapters, I will go over what I learned and hope you find it useful.

Chapter 2: Over-achiever mindset –The Go Getter

I really identified with Joe from **The Go-Giver** as he went through his transformations. I was brought up believing that you could achieve anything through hard work. Of course, it also required education, otherwise manual labor positions would be near the top of the pay scale. With two parents in academia, it also wasn't about who was the smartest or had the most education. In the corporate world, it was about being efficient with your time because there was only so much you could get done in a day. David Allen was my hero with his book, **Getting Things Done**. I was the quintessential go getter. Get out of my way or I'd walk up your back. I was too shy to be a total asshole, but I didn't always possess the greatest patience in the world. I remember one annual review that mentioned my lack of patience with people that weren't as smart as me. Time was precious and so I didn't want to waste time with niceties if we were supposed to be getting things done. If you can't keep up, take notes as one of my friends is fond of saying.

The scarcity belief that there was never enough time transferred over to their never being enough money. I started to become aware that everything is connected. I didn't have enough energy to get everything done that I wanted to in order to make the amount of money that I wanted. It was the classical have-do-be paradox. After I had what I needed, I could do what I wanted and be who I wanted to be. In order to keep going day after day at 100% efficiency, I numbed out my emotions. By putting down the things I wanted to remember to get done on lists, I could empty my mind enough to get to sleep. Before starting that, I would have to shut down with alcohol and mind numbing TV. If I tried to read a book, I'd just fall asleep and then wake up in an anxious panic in the middle of the night. It wasn't until I discovered the magic of meditation that I finally figured out to make peace with my mind and its endless running thoughts.

Even with my desire to get things done and make a difference in the world, I was an empathic person that liked to make other people happy. I was turned off by the prototypical driven business person that put themselves first and treated everyone else like crap. As a manager, I was constantly fighting for recognition for the accomplishments of the team and trying my best to get promotions for the individual team members. I did tend to expect big things from those above me in the management chain. I didn't see myself as an outwardly egotistical person. I was confused by all the references to ego in the self-help and spiritual work. It wasn't until I recognized that my ego wasn't one that had me strutting around like a peacock. My ego was what drew me into fights to prove that I was right on occasion or had me trying to prove my worth. Awareness in that area led me to ask better questions and focus on helping people. The idea of servant leadership really resonated with me. I loved the concepts in **Leadershift** by Orrin Woodward and Oliver DeMille. I was also attracted to the Rotary motto of "Service above self."

So, now, I believed that I solved the problem of my ego. Until, I realized that I had awareness of my ego's outward tendencies and practiced techniques to keep it in check, yet my ego had an even larger impact on me when it turned inward. My ego is focused on perfection. It is a perfect critic. It was the noise in my head I was trying to numb out, not my emotions. Unfortunately, I was numbing out my emotions rather than realizing it was my ego that was making me feel miserable and less than. Stories that resonated with me and woke me up showed me that rather than feeling the heat of the stove, I had injected Novocain into my fingertips. Actually a more relevant story had me walking on a path over broken glass when there was a path with nice soft grass running parallel. By taking a deep breath and a moment to relax, I started to practice listening to my intuition. You know that gut feeling that gives you guidance that you often mull over endlessly in your mind. I would often tie myself in knots over thinking things and then just ask someone else, rather than trusting myself. Slowly, I began to value my own intuition and follow it.

When I start to slide back into scarcity thinking, I still miss the perceived certainty that hard work would bring the success I was seeking. It was a big part of my identity to know that I could walk over broken glass longer than almost anyone else. Yeah me!!! My ability to achieve was the old miserable me. The new me is much happier and more fun to be around. What a powerful thing, to find your purpose and start taking intention action.

Chapter 3: Entrepreneurs – The Big Leap

It was time to declare my freedom. Being responsible for generating my own income took quite a leap of faith. Moving into the entrepreneurial side, I see many people, including myself initially, working even harder in their own businesses than they did before. To others, running your own business looks like hard work. Sometimes, it feels like hard work, especially early on when I didn't see the results yet. It does take energy to build your dream. Luckily, I found there is an infinite supply of energy for me to tap into when I am doing what I love. Of course, I have to make time to re-charge, re-shape my vision and learn lessons. I found the book **The Big Leap** by Gay Hendricks to be a great introduction to what it takes to be an entrepreneur.

Business is a game of power, not force. Many of the corporate pep talks I've been subjected to are based on military themes. I don't know how many Sun Tzu, **Art of War** quotes I've heard at annual sales meetings or all-hands company meetings. I realize it was an attempt to motivate the troops to soldier on for the good of the company. I usually rolled my eyes and made fun of them. Now, I realize why I didn't resonate with the message. I didn't want to be led into battle. I wanted to be inspired, not motivated. I wanted to know how we were going to change the world. Often, that is now lost in the corporate world of quarterly market reports. Motivation is force. Inspiration is power.

Force-based tactics only take you so far, which is why so many big companies have disappeared or become irrelevant over time. True power comes from serving your clients, not conquering them. Entrepreneurs learn this very quickly or fail just as quickly when making the leap from the corporate world. The name of the game is about creating value in the eyes of your client, not trying to prove your worth. It is about inviting and enrolling them to your mission, not manipulating them into buying something.

Changing the world requires power, which is why the entrepreneurial movement is building so much momentum. It is a game with no losers. Entrepreneurs are doing what they love and find easy for others that don't mind exchanging for value since they have a different passion. No one gets taken advantage of, at least not for long. The market quickly exposes people not delivering value. There is no rationalizing that it is "just business" when someone is harmed or the environment is damaged. Everyone must win for lasting change. Force can take the hilltop. Power brings peace.

The world is a complicated place and is constantly changing. You can't control all the variables. Science and engineering over-simplify specific tests to seek out cause and effect relationships. More and more, chaos theory or quantum physics show that these simplified models don't help us with real life. Trying to predict the future and even the specifics of a given day is to fight a losing battle. Entrepreneurs realize that whatever comes along, they can handle it. Since you can't control the cause, all you can control is your response. Not having to worry about trying to control everything relieves a lot of meaningless stress. Life as an entrepreneur is all about freedom, which is great since one of my core values is freedom. You are free to do things your way with the people you choose. You control your time and don't have to trade time for money. You can choose what you do today. You are free to create something each and every day, so please get to it. Not because you have to but because you want to.

The freedom of choice goes hand in hand with the next principle, which is taking 100% responsibility. This concept also relates back to the topic of power versus force. What is more powerful, the person blaming everyone else from the president to the economy to the weather for the state of their business or the person taking responsibility for what happened and working to make it better for all involved? I hope the answer is obvious. When things don't work out in a preferred way, learn the lesson or it will be even more painful when it happens again. Blaming others just makes you the victim and that is most powerless position to be in. Feeling justified in fighting back after someone wronged you is how many feuds, battles and wars have been started. If each participant takes full responsibility regardless of what the other participants do, the world would be a much more peaceful place.

Fortunately, entrepreneurs can truly throw away the work/life balance question for a both-AND. An OR choice implies giving something up while using AND doesn't. Work and life are the same, not separate compartments of my life, so it is not work or life but work and life. I can sleep eight hours a night, have a happy family, create value for others and except currency in exchange. I get to do what comes easy for me and find my niche. I don't have to worry about being replaced by someone else's idea of an ideal job description or someone who is willing to sacrifice more life for work. I have the ability to choose who I work with, set my pace and find my rhythm.

Every evening as I put down my work for the day to spend time with my top priority, my family and friends, I reflect back on the day. What went well? What lessons did I become aware of? What am I going to do tomorrow to make it even better? Now, I go home without distractions. The next morning, I meditate, read or listen to something inspiration, write in my journal, then jump onto my top priorities first, while I'm re-charged, revved up and clear.

Of course, the life of an entrepreneur is not always this idealistic tale. It can be extremely frustrating when the same lesson is being taught to you over and over again without it coming through to you. We can't all be Thomas Edison and fail 10,000 times before figuring out how to accomplish the task at hand. Another one of my core values is collaboration because you can't see the picture frame when you are in the picture. It is important to surround yourself with others willing to help lift you up while keeping you grounded. These same people can often see what you are missing if you are willing to ask for help. If you haven't been a business owner your entire life, it can be a lonely place when you realize that most of your friends have no idea what you are dealing with. You need to find your tribe or community of like-minded business owners so you can help each other overcome the inevitable obstacles that are going to need overcoming. Actually, a big help is to not look at them as obstacles or challenges at all, but as opportunities for growth and expansion.

Chapter 4: Finding flow – The Effortless Effort

It's been called a lot of things. That feeling when things are just working out for you. Athletes call it being in the zone. Things seem to slow down and become very clear. You amaze even yourself with what you are doing. Can you remember the last time you were in flow? What did it feel like? Did it feel hard or like a huge effort? You may have been drained afterwards, both physically and mentally, but also fulfilled with a feeling of meaningful accomplishment. Imagine the feeling of forming a daily habit of getting in flow.

Many entrepreneurs struggle with the social programming that work has to be hard. They have this understanding that it is hard to make money. This feeling that if money comes too easily it has not been earned. Another common belief is that it is hard or at least uncomfortable to ask for money for your services. I hear many people undercut themselves, while secretly hoping that the client will so love the service that they generously offer more money. A common method to avoid the discomfort is to try and trade services. Unfortunately, this is not usually an efficient and effective strategy. You can't pay the mortgage with an IOU for a massage. You can't cash a coupon for a car detailing at the grocery store. Currency was created by some extremely smart people to create an efficient barter tool. You don't have to accept chickens from the farmer for fixing his roof, and then trade the chickens to the baker for some bread. A direct barter system rarely is more efficient than an exchange of value based on a commonly agreed on currency, whether that is dollar bills, colored shells or beads.

With that said, it is tough to keep in mind that currency is just a tool. It is a tool allowing for our current global economy. We tend to forget the difference between currency and money. Currency is a tool and money is our inherent value we bring to the marketplace. It is easy to test the truth of this statement. Imagine that I'm handing a check for $1,000,000. How do you feel? Now, I snatch it back and rip it up. Do you revert back to the same feeling you had before you initially received it or is there a sense of loss? For most of us, we can rationalize the fact we are back to where we started but we have a hard time letting go of the feeling of how life was going to be different when we had $1,000,000 a few seconds ago.

It is tough to keep using currency in place of the more commonly used money. A simple distinction is that there is no value behind a dollar bill other than the socially agreed on tool of commerce. This paper is often portrayed as a symbol for a better life. After this paragraph, I'll revert to using money and currency interchangeably for readability. For the next few sentences, I'll try to better illustrate my point by keeping them distinctly separate. I see this attachment to currency show up in many ways. Say you earned the big check mentioned above for doing something that hurt others or damaged the environment in some way. Again, some rationalization is required to keep the guilt down. Statements like "if I hadn't done it, someone else would have?" or "the ends justify the means." I'd say this is more common in the corporate or criminal worlds. In the entrepreneurial world, it is more common to not allow yourself to accept the true value that you are bringing to the world. Of course, any of these arguments are not that important in the larger scheme of things. How much would a dying parent pay for the ability to see their children get married or meet their grandchildren? What would you do with a million dollars in cash out in the middle of the Sahara desert? It is tough to keep the fear, doubt and worry that we feel about not having enough currency in perspective. As the saying goes, money can't buy you love. However, currency can buy you a lot of things to numb out feelings of lack or unworthiness.

There is a tendency to focus on lack that tends to hold us back. There never seems to be enough time in the day or enough money to do what we really want or the energy to keep going on like this forever. Does that sound familiar? It seems be the default human condition to focus on what is lacking and falling back into scarcity. Focusing on creating value is a much more productive pursuit. Being creative and finding yourself in flow means you are more fulfilled at the end of the day. Trying to grind through all the mundane things that you believe you should be doing drains your most important commodity, energy. Doing something that you love boosts your energy, which means you get more done in less time. It is a small shift in mindset, yet it is amazingly powerful. It really illustrates how mind, body and spirit are all connected.

As you find yourself in the habit of having fun and being creative, suddenly the world opens up and things really start happening. For many followers of transformational leaders, this is the Shangri-La that they keep hoping for by using positive affirmations and vision boards. For entrepreneurs, it is the tipping point they keep pushing for where suddenly they have enough money and time to do what they really want to. Of course, to really get there, it is helpful to stop pushing. You intuitively know the answer already. If you follow someone else's system or method, it will not be your own. Again, a subtle shift in mindset is all that it takes. Allow yourself to accept your true value in exchange for the service that you provide. Don't sabotage yourself. A helpful tool is to focus on asking powerful questions and inviting potential clients to join your mission. As you are talking to people, make sure you're making some sort of offer before closing. Is it more polite to invite yourself or simply accept an invitation if you are interested in the other person?

The key point to remember is that value lies in the eyes of the other. How can you know what they value? By asking, of course. Before telling them about how great your product or service is, it is helpful to know if they value what it is that you are about to vomit all over them. Okay, that's a little gross, but you know what I'm talking about. You love what you do and you want everyone to experience it. Standard advertising is about manipulating people into wanting what is being sold. That can work for products. Most entrepreneurs are selling themselves more than a product. Refuse to be commoditized. There is someone that is seeking exactly what it is that you do. Out of good stewardship for their money, they will try to commoditize you. By being focused and intentional on exactly what value you bring to the marketplace, you not only won't be commoditized but you'll create raving fans out of your clients. They'll tell all their friends and family about how incredible you are. Now, how hard is it to ask for those personal introductions to the next client for you to serve? I'm smiling now as I write this because it is easy to say but often hard to do. Something I find useful is to keep in mind that you know you've found your niche when you are creating value at more than $1,000 per hour. Focus on those activities that create value. The other stuff you can take care of later or delegate to someone else, even if they don't exist yet. The important thing is not to trade time for money. That is a job. You are an entrepreneur. You can use leverage. This is how you create more money and more time.

Chapter 5: You see the world as you are – being with Stairway of Selves

If you are like I was, now you are excited because I just said "how" it could be done. Psych. Getting stuck in the "how" is what held me back for so long. I'd have an exciting idea and immediately start trying to implement it in my head. I'd spin around and around in my head. Chewing on that unsolvable problem would keep me up at night. I'd play the "what if" game, usually spinning down all the reasons why it wouldn't work until it was just easier to give up. Trying to find ways out of the trap of a cushy salary in the corporate world that made you miserable is usually stymied by how I am going to keep my family in the lifestyle they are accustomed to. I didn't realize that I was my own worst enemy.

As humans, we create our own reality. We see the world as we are. In **Power vs Force**, Dr. David Hawkins really digs into the details of how powerful we are as we allow ourselves to rise to a higher level of consciousness. Uh oh, I'm going off the new age deep end. Seriously though, whatever your religious or spiritual beliefs, the teachings are all very similar. True happiness is living a life of peace and love. How is this applicable in the cut throat world of business? Don't take my word for it, just take a look around at some of the people that you admire and consider successful. Are they the all work and no play types, manically working on the project of the moment. Are they focused solely on making the most money possible? Are they bitter and complaining about how unfair life is? My question to you is, what comes first, the success and then the attitude, or the success as the result of the attitude?

Napoleon Hill in **Think and Grow Rich** makes a strong case for attitude is the key. Take a look at the **Stairway of Selves** graphic, borrowed from Steve D'Annunzio. When you are down in the physical realm, is it any wonder you're not making the money and building the relationships you want? You are predominantly in flight or fight mode all the time. I see most of the cut throat business world operating in the lower half of the mental realm, still in fear versus love mode. People and businesses make money at this level but it is an ego dominated existence. This is the land of expensive suits, cars and watches, where each person is trying to outdo the others. It is common to find people burning out or getting divorced, while hoping that the next big break will truly make them happy.

Joy Level		Life-View	GOD-SELF	Life Results	Power Level	
	99%	Sacred	UNCONDITIONAL LOVE	Divine	100,000,000 watts	
	97%	Perfect	LOVE	Revelatory	10,000,000 watts	
	91%	Serene	WISDOM	Transcendent	1,000,000 watts	
	85%	Understanding	ACCEPTANCE	Fulfilled	500,000 watts	
	77%	Hopeful	REASON	Creative	50,000 watts	
TRUTH	60%	Empowered	COURAGE	Positive	10,000 watts	LOVE
FALSEHOOD	32%	Controlling	PRIDE	Enslaved	1,000 watts	FEAR
	21%	Blaming	ENTITLEMENT	Disappointing	500 watts	
	18%	Punishing	ANGER	Disease	100 watts	
	15%	Unfulfilled	DESIRE	Wanting	75 watts	
	12%	Frightening	FEAR	Fighting	60 watts	
	5%	Miserable	VICTIM	Poverty	30 watts	

Physical Realm   Mental Realm   Spiritual Realm

Used by Permission of Steve D'Annunzio, missiondrivenadvisor.com

When people are below the midline, the low level of consciousness creates a low level result, in money and relationships. People are rarely happy and struggle to keep up. Of course, the blame goes outside themselves. It is about proving your worth, while chopping down those around you so that you feel taller. You often see people that are setting out to make others wrong. People on top tell others below them what they should be doing. Those lower down on the corporate food chain often rebel. The big change comes as you crossover the lower stairs where people are stuck in fear to one of more awareness. Rather than blaming everyone else, you realize that everyone is doing the best they can and that you are your own biggest asset. It is important to invest in yourself, through education, self-improvement and overall wellness. If you ask someone what they want in life enough times, eventually they get to the point of saying, "I just want to be happy". "Pursuit of Happiness" is a core value of most Americans since it is written in to the Declaration of Independence. The true brilliance of that statement didn't fully hit me until I heard a discussion about the meaning of these three words. Most of us think it means that it is our right to chase after whatever makes us happy. At the time, it more likely meant something akin to the right to practice well-being. It resonates much more with me to say that I have the right to be happy rather than constantly chasing after happiness.

The eye opener for me was in moving beyond fear. An entrepreneur, or any business owner for that matter, must make decisions every day to move the business forward. In government or large corporations, it seems to be acceptable to suffer analysis paralysis by asking for more data, doing a survey or forming a committee to consider all the angles before making any BIG decision. For them, it is seen as prudent to question everything until the decisions make themselves or the situation changes to where no decision is required. If I'm right, which I'm not claiming, it might explain the state of the nation right now. True leadership is about making the best decision possible with the data available. In life, most decisions are not black and white, but somewhere in the shades of gray. For an entrepreneur, moving in any direction, even if it is totally in the wrong way, is better than sitting still, or worse, madly spinning around and around. The world is constantly changing. If you are not changing with it, you are contracting rather than expanding.

So why is it that we constantly find ourselves in a state of fear of a looming BIG decision and how can we push through it. I resonate with the explanation that much of the fear comes from the reptilian portion of our brain. Early in human history, a mostly hairless, two-legged mammal had a lot to be afraid of. The shadow in a corner might actually be hiding something that could eat us. Nowadays, it is more likely nothing or just the family cat. Much of the fear we feel is not real, just our brain trying to protect us as it always has. While most business decisions are obviously not life or death, our brain still tends to focus first on all the things that might go wrong in order to keep us safe. What if it all goes horribly wrong, then we can't pay the mortgage or feed the kids or put gas in the car, then everyone in our family hates us and leaves us all alone? I call it the "what if" game. I used to spiral down from some big hairy decisions into a state of analysis paralysis, playing it safe because the wrong decision could have horrible consequences. Eventually, I learned that you could play the "what if" game to consciously spiral upward. What if everything worked out for me and I was exactly in the right place at the right time? Playing it safe would not allow me to reach my true potential and make the difference in the world I was meant to.

Pushing through the fear is not always easy. First, it is important to realize where the fear is coming from. It is my ego trying to keep me safe. Thank you ego, I really appreciate you helping me. However, I really don't think picking up the phone to call a business owner from an email introduction is a life or death decision for me. What if I blow it? Instead, what if I really connect with him or her? Maybe I should write a blog post or update my web page instead. No. My intuition is telling me that now is the best time to reach out. Rationally, I'm aware that I don't control the outcome of the call, just whether I dial or not. That still doesn't keep my palms from sweating. I should straighten my desk or go to the bathroom, maybe a cup of coffee first. Stop!!! Take a deep breath. Pick up the phone and dial. Now, just let things flow.

Okay, the story above is a bit of an overblown example just to make a point. Most BIG decisions can be broken down into a series of smaller decisions where the negative consequences are just as silly. For really serious decisions, it is important to check in with what your intuition is telling you, what your rational mind is saying and what your ego is saying. If your gut says go for it, you rationally see that it aligns with your mission and your ego is saying "wait, this is too scary", congratulations you have made a great decision. Go for it. You'll learn a lot.

If you still aren't convinced that many of the negative thoughts you focus on are the same ones holding you back, let's try another approach. I had a real "ah-ha" moment during a discussion of what it meant to be present, not stuck in the past or fast-forwarding to the future. Right here, right now, are you safe or is something about to eat you? If you catch yourself thinking about stuff you woulda, coulda or shoulda done after feeling guilt or shame, you are stuck in the past. If you are anxious with fear, doubt and worry, then you are stuck in the future. Name what you are feeling and assess whether you are really in danger right now or whether it is just your thoughts trying to protect you. If you are having trouble moving beyond, try to release the thought to the universe. Releasing is helpful to keep from getting stuck. Big things may keep coming back until you can really forgive yourself or others. Rather than focusing on who did what or whose fault it is, have compassion for others. Everyone is doing the best they can. For many of us, the person we need to have the most compassion for is ourselves.

Chapter 6: Prioritize merged work/life activities – take intentional action

Most business books are all about taking action. Here we are at the last chapter and finally the topic is broached. That is because most of the time we get it backwards. We think that if we have something (more time, more money, better relationships), then they can do something (write a book, start a new hobby, go on a dream vacation) and then we can be something (happy, fulfilled, loved). It is not about activity but productivity. It is about whom you are being, leading to what you are doing and resulting in all you wanted to have. It comes down to having faith in yourself. When you are in touch with your core values and doing things that light you up, then things just have a way of working out for you. You only know two things for certain, that you were born and that someday you'll leave this physical form. Everything else has some amount of uncertainty to it. Rather than spending your life worrying about all the things that could go wrong or that have gone wrong, be the best version of yourself each and every day. This means tending to your mind, body and spirit. Do you identify more with a physical being having a spiritual experience or a spiritual being have a physical experience? If it is the later, you are here for a reason, so why not go for it?

This doesn't mean that you live like every day is your last day. It is about finding a balance that works for you. It means taking inspired action in case this is your last day or you live to over 100 years old. It means doing something important for your life and your business. I've found resonance in understanding that discipline is freedom. By building up habits to nurture your mind, body and spirit, they become automatic. You don't find yourself procrastinating the really important things but doing them first. It allows you to live in appreciation each day without guilt. For example, if you are habitually saving 15%, who cares if you want to buy a nice watch or pair of shoes? If you exercised for an hour, who cares if you sit on the couch and watch an hour of television?

The important thing is to build up to it, not attempt to make complete changes over night. That is one reason why diets don't work. It is about doing 1% more in all phases of your life each day and every day. You don't go run a marathon the first day you start working out. You don't cut out all fat and carbs on the first day of a new eating routine. You don't try to meditate for an hour your first time. Go for a walk around the neighborhood for fifteen minutes, have one less beer or glass of wine with dinner, meditate for 1 minute. Get it? Gradual changes, each and every day and by the end of the year, you'll have come full circle, a full 360 degrees. We often over-estimate the amount we can get done in a day and way under-estimate how much we can get done in a year.

Another thing that helped me was around the concept of keeping score. I grew up in a household where nothing was ever good enough or at least the question was how you are going to do it better next time? At the end of you day, rather than focusing on what you didn't get done, focus on what you did. Celebrate what you did do rather beat yourself up for what you didn't. When planning for the next day, what are the things that would mean the most to you, if you accomplished them? If you have 10 phone calls to make, start with the scariest one first because it probably is the one that is the most meaningful. Even before starting the work day, I found that by spending time meditating, writing in a journal and reading inspirational stuff before everyone else gets up, after at least eight hours of sleep, gave me more energy to handle everything the rest of the day. Before adding the extra hour to the start of my day, I'd jump out of bed and into the shower, scramble to make lunches and get the kids on the bus and rush off to the office. I'd be frazzled and irritable as I started my work day, not an ideal state to be in. I also found that by me being calm and collected, it helped the rest of the family as well. We now find time to eat breakfast rather grabbing a granola bar and banana on the way out the door. The inevitable closet full of ping pong balls is waiting at the office, as soon as I open the door. It helped me to build habits to work on the important things first before getting overwhelmed with emails, especially when I plan them the day before. It feels good to spend 15-30 minutes celebrating the victories of the day and planning for tomorrow as the last thing I do in the office. I am then fully present at home, especially after I replaced listening to the world's problems on NPR with entrepreneurial podcasts on the drive home. The feeling of constantly running on the hamster wheel is replaced with a clarity and sense of purpose. I can have a wonderful family life and a successful business.

Of course, forming new habits is not always a smooth ride. Your ego will try to convince you to hit snooze a few times rather than getting up to do your new morning routine. The boys or girls will want you stay for one more drink. The more subtle area where it helps to surround yourself with like-minded people is in changing the core of who you are being. Most of us default to scarcity thinking when we stop being present. There is not enough time, money or energy. We make excuses or outright sabotage ourselves. It is tough to change your belief system because you've lived in the story for so long. Find an accountability partner or group because they will see right away where you are holding yourself back. The best advice I heard was not to judge. When you start telling people what they should be doing, most likely you have fallen back into an old mode of being. Also, keep telling yourself that change is inevitable so you have to keep expanding. Get comfortable with being uncomfortable. Otherwise, you are not growing with the changes. I loved hearing my son repeat back something I'd told him to my daughter as they were learning to ski. He told her that if she wasn't falling, then she wasn't pushing herself to learn more. That is a good message to have on the bathroom mirror. We don't ever chide the toddler learning to walk for being unsteady. We encourage them to keep trying because we know they can do it.

As a final thought, it helps to be aware that things may not work exactly as you plan. There are no failures, only lessons. The tough part is that if you don't learn the lesson, each one keeps getting tougher every time. It helps to maintain a childlike curiosity and keep questioning. Trying new things doesn't always mean that you are adding more things to your pile of stuff to do. Sometimes, it is about stopping something that you've always done. The term that sticks with me is "addition by subtraction". If you take off a backpack full of 20 pounds of rock, do you think you could run faster and farther? Enjoy life's journey, you are doing great.

Epilogue

Thanks for reading my first book. I hope you found parts of it useful. Depending on where you are right now in your life, you will take away different things each time you read it. If you found value in this book, please let others know about it. A big reason why I formed The Entrepreneurs' Collaborative Network was to help "pay it forward" by connecting people together that are in business for all the right reasons.

The byproduct is that I keep learning as I coach others to unlock the true value of their business. By speaking at various events, I keep meeting incredibly interesting people. As I blog each week, I explore things in my own transformation. To find what I'm up to now, check out my website www.dantgardner.com.

Appendix: 8-step program

For those of you that finished the book and are looking for more practical steps to start transforming your own life and business, this appendix has an overview of the initial topics I go through when starting a coaching program with a business owner looking to make the next big leap. Take a look and let me know when you are ready to get started. You can do it on your own. Using a coach, you can do it so much faster.

Step 1 – Relax

Relax, take a deep breath. Expel the fear, doubt and worry. That is all about a future not yet decided. Get rid of the woulda, coulda, shoulda stuff. That is all in the past, no need for guilt or shame. You are safe now. Be present. You are supported by those around you. Now, ask yourself what is out of balance in your life? Are you working too much that your family and friends are feeling left out? Are you not making the money you want in order to hire people to help offload the things you don't enjoy doing? Listen to the answer and write it down. I find most people are holding themselves back somewhere with scarcity beliefs. Welcome to entrepreneurship.

What are three things in your life and business that would make this the best month, six months or year ever, if they happened? What is holding you back? Again, write the answers down.

Step 2 – Find or remember your purpose

Think back to why you started your business? How has it evolved? Initially, you were probably just trying to put food on the table, replace a job. As you surpass survival, you start to realize there is purpose bigger than yourself. It has to do with serving others and helping to relieve suffering. What is your why (write it down)? Lead with this intention at the start to every meeting.

Step 3 – Continue to expand

If you are in alignment with your purpose, you have found something that you enjoy doing, are quite good at, others value and you are willing continue to work towards mastery. If you aren't expanding, you are contracting. It is important to continue to study your craft: read, listen to podcasts, go to seminars, hang out with other liked-minded people, work with coaches, etc. This is a step that many disciples of new age thinking miss. It is not about sitting back and waiting for things to come to you. It is that the effort doesn't feel like hard work to you whereas it would for others not in alignment with their purpose.

Step 4 – Ask powerful questions

How many of you feel you are quite expert in the area of your business? Do you find yourself just going for it and trying to educate people about all the stuff you know? How does that work? Probably, totally hit or miss with a lot of wasted time. People don't care how much you know until they know how much you care. In addition, if they have no interest in what you do, how much are they going to value the conversation? So before you launch into your new sales presentation and vomit features and benefits all over them, take some time to ask powerful questions. The idea is to not be doing all the talking. Telling is selling. Serving is about creating value in the client's eyes. Don't get stuck trying to prove your worth. Open ended "what" questions tend to give you the most information about how the person currently is feeling. You can tailor them to better fit your specific niche. The basic questions are of the form:

> Where are you at?
> Where do you want to be?
> What's in the way?

Step 5 – Make offers

In sales, you are taught about prospecting as a way to get new clients. It is the dreaded cold calls or endless networking meetings. The key to making it more fun is shift the mindset from one of prospecting to one of inviting. My preference is that if there is a fit between what I do and what you are looking for that we work together. I'm not attached, which doesn't mean I don't care. It just means that I'm okay with no, not right now or even no, not ever. Think of a waiter at a cocktail party offering up a crab cake. The waiter doesn't go back to the kitchen and cry because you didn't want a crab cake right then. They'll probably even come back around in about 5 minutes and try to convince you to accept the tasty crab cake again, or the food on the plate is different this time around. The key is to be inviting people to connect with you in some way. If there is no offer, then the other person isn't quite sure what to do. Should they invite themselves or wait for an invitation from you? It really ties into the previous step. If you have asked them what they value and you can help, then ask them to connect.

The key is to build trust by inviting them to have a conversation where you can ask questions to diagnose the issues. The offer is then customized to what they care about and all you are doing is enrolling them into your process and asking them if they are ready to take action. If there is no commitment to change on the other side, you will not be successful. You can't want it more than they do. People don't want to be sold but they love to buy. Especially when the product is you, people don't realize what they really need. They want something. Assuming you can diagnose this area better than they can, you come back with the prescription. Even with products, it helps to ask enough questions to find out what the perceived need is, the level of knowledge around the subject and the commitment to take action.

Step 6 – Introductions

Do you wait to ask for referrals until after closing a sale? Do you even ask at all? Do you feel comfortable or uncomfortable? Remember the mindset of inviting versus making the person invite themselves. Imagine you've connected with someone, found out quite a bit about them and now realize that your products and services are not a good fit for this person right now. How hard would it be to say? It was really great meeting you and enjoyed getting to know you. It appears that I'm not the right fit right now for you. You now have a pretty good idea of how I do business even though we haven't transacted in any way. What would it take for me to be referable in your eyes? What is the worst thing they can say? I love asking this question during an initial meet and greet networking event or during an initial conversation with a prospective client. Sometimes, they graciously say, "You already are." I graciously thank them and ask them to set the bar a bit higher. I say something like, "If we were to work together, what would we need to accomplish to make you a raving fan?" How hard is it now to go back and ask for the introduction when you've done exactly that?

Step 7 – Make time

Do you catch yourself in scarcity around time? I don't have time to do this or that. I don't time for lunch. If a child, especially your own, walked in the room right now with a nail through their foot, would you make time to take them to the emergency room. Of course you would. Don't be a victim of your own schedule. Make time for the most important person in your life. YOU!!! Skip that late night TV show so you can get up 30 minutes earlier and meditate, talk a walk, or read that inspirational book first thing in the morning. We tend to procrastinate doing the things we really don't like doing until we are motivated by stress to get them done just in time for a deadline. This also drains our energy. I don't know about you but when I'm putting off doing something I don't really want to do, that is when I clean my desk or rearrange my sock drawer. Not exactly great uses of time either. Instead, working on those inspirational and creative things that really differentiate your business actually get done faster first thing in the morning and often give us an energy boost, allowing us to do the other tasks that we don't find so much fun. Time flies when you are in the zone, doing the things you love. Do that one thing that will really move you first thing, then let the rest of the day happen. I find it helpful to plan out that one thing the day before as I close out my work day and transition into family mode. I spend about fifteen minutes before leaving the office scheduling out all the things that absolutely must get done the next day and that helps get it out of my head.

Step 8 – Discipline is freedom

The paragraph above can be akin to eating your dessert first. You may have early morning meetings that are difficult to change or that make it impossible to spend the first hour of the day powering you up. You have routines with kids or spouses that have become habit at night making it hard to change your time tables to make more time for yourself. It is not about making huge changes all at once. That is more like going on a diet. You may stick to it for a while but eventually it is just too hard. Give yourself a break. Take control of your life and stop being the victim of your own excuses. Try to do 1% more in all phases of your life each day. After a year, you'll have come full circle. For example, maybe you want to try meditation and get more exercise. Start with meditating one minute tomorrow morning. Park your car 10 spaces further away from the office or take the stairs. Everybody is different and yet we are all the same. Find something that works for you. Discipline is freedom. Plan out what is really important to you and do it first. Who cares how much time you waste later? Amazingly though, you'll get it all done or figure out what wasn't really that important to get it done in the first place. By embracing your creativity, you'll find you are more productive and can start offloading other tasks to others. When you are in flow, you will be earning $1000 or more per hour, so doing a $20 an hour task is costing you at least $980. How would it feel to be make time for yourself and the people you love, yet be more productive than ever?